THE COMPLETE PIANO PLAYER
BOOK 3

'By the end of this book you will understand
the importance of expression in music,
and will be playing 22 popular songs,
including: *Imagine, Blue Moon, Norwegian Wood,*
and *Raindrops Keep Falling On My Head.*'

Kenneth Baker

Book designed by Howard Brown
Book photography by Peter Wood

Order No. AM34844
Printed in the EU

ISBN: 978-0-7119-0433-2

HAL•LEONARD®

Copyright © 1984, 1993 by Wise Publications

No part of this publication may be reproduced in any form or by
any means without the prior written permission of the Publisher.

Visit Hal Leonard Online at
www.halleonard.com

Contact us:
Hal Leonard
7777 West Bluemound Road
Milwaukee, WI 53213
Email: info@halleonard.com

In Europe, contact:
Hal Leonard Europe Limited
42 Wigmore Street
Marylebone, London, W1U 2RY
Email: info@halleonardeurope.com

In Australia, contact:
Hal Leonard Australia Pty. Ltd.
4 Lentara Court
Cheltenham, Victoria, 3192 Australia
Email: info@halleonard.com.au

CONTENTS

About this book, 5

LESSONS

1. Chord pyramids, 6
   'Shift' technique, 7
   Chord pyramids for right hand, 8
2. New notes: G, A, and Low B for right hand, 10
   F, G, A, B for left hand, 10
   Accompaniment patterns, 10
3. Phrasing, 12
4. Key of G, Scale of G, 14
5. $\frac{6}{8}$ Time, 16
6. The two-note slur, 18
7. New note: High D for left hand, 20
8. Arpeggio (broken chord) style for left hand, 22
9. Semiquavers (sixteenth notes), 24
10. The Waltz, 26
    Da Capo al Coda, 27
11. Grace notes, 28
    Acciaccatura, 29
12. Accidentals, 30
13. Repeated notes, 32
14. Semiquavers (sixteenth notes) in $\frac{4}{4}$ Time, 34
15. New notes: B, C for right hand, High E for left hand, 36
16. Triplets, 38
    Arpeggio (broken chord) style for both hands, 38
17. Crotchet (quarter note) triplet, 40
18. More left hand melody playing, 42
19. The Dotted Quaver (Dotted Eighth Note), 44
20. Swing, 46
    Last word, 48

SONGS

Amazing Grace, 39
Blue Moon, 14
Dream Baby, 12
Fascination, 8
Greensleeves, 17
I'm Not In Love, 42
Imagine, 34
Irish Washerwoman, 32
Lawrence Of Arabia (Theme from), 40
Liberty Bell, 20
Minuet in G, 36
Morning (from Peer Gynt), 24
Norwegian Wood, 18
Ob-La-Di, Ob-La-Da, 28
Over The Rainbow, 30
Raindrops Keep Falling On My Head, 46
Smile, 6
Somewhere My Love, 26
Spanish Eyes, 10
Summer Place (A) (Theme from), 22
Wonder Of You (The), 48
Yellow Submarine, 45

ABOUT THIS BOOK

Now that you have successfully completed the first two books of The Complete Piano Player, you are ready to learn some styles which will make you "sound like a professional".

As before, all lessons are based on songs made famous by outstanding groups and stars, as well as on delightful classical pieces. Altogether there are twenty new songs and pieces to add to your already considerable repertoire.

You will also get plenty of practice in note reading, and your sense of timing and rhythm will become even more developed. Easy to follow text and clear diagrams, as usual, ensure that your progress is made as smooth as possible.

If you are working on your own, keep up regular practice every day. This is the way to achieve your aim of becoming a complete piano player.

TO TEACHERS

Book Three of The Complete Piano Player course follows the proven principles laid down in the first two books. Sound technique is taught throughout. Lessons are made enjoyable by basing them on music which keeps students interested throughout the entire course. As a course for teaching today's students, you will find The Complete Piano Player ideal.

CHORD PYRAMIDS

This is a simple yet effective type of accompaniment which can be used with most ballads (slow expressive tunes, often played with a rather flexible tempo).

Play the notes of the chord one by one with your left hand, holding each note down until the chord pyramid is formed. Observe the ties carefully.

SMILE

Words: John Turner & Geoffrey Parsons. Music: Charles Chaplin

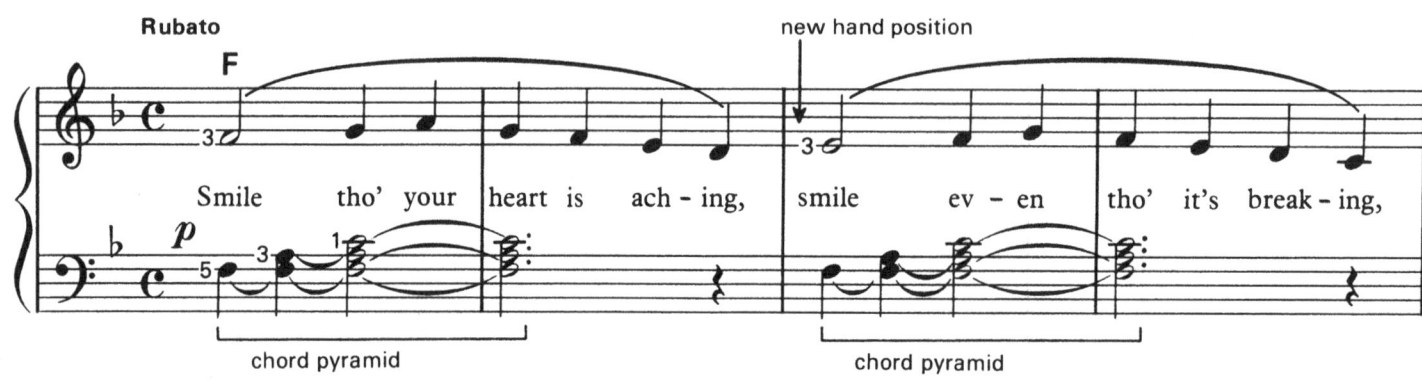

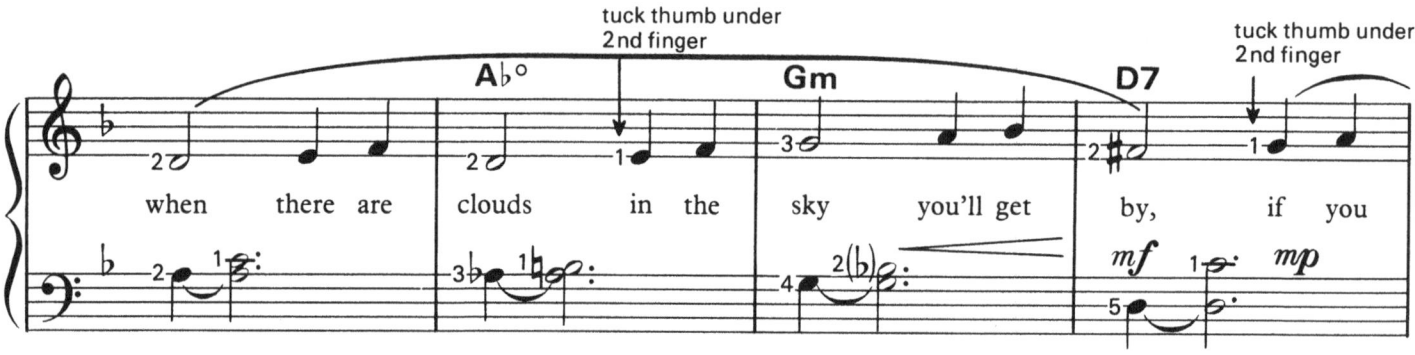

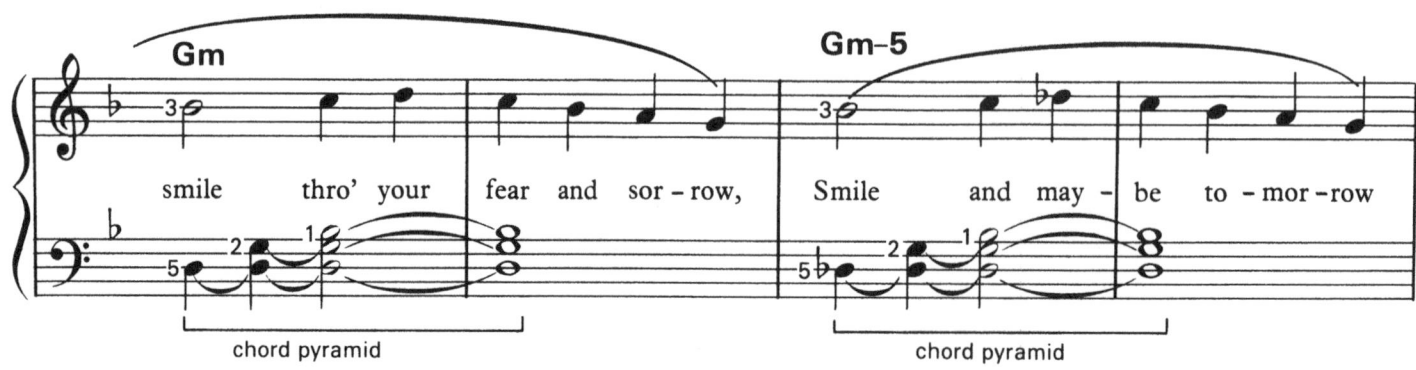

***Shift Technique.** Sometimes necessary for good legato playing. Play F with 3rd finger then shift to 5th finger without releasing the note. The 3rd finger is now ready for use again in the next phrase.

© Copyright 1954 by Bourne Inc., USA. Bourne Music Ltd., for the British Commonwealth of Nations (exc. Canada & Australasia) and Eire.
All rights reserved. International copyright secured.

The chord pyramid technique can often be used effectively in the right hand also, as seen in the following arrangement of *Fascination*.

FASCINATION

Music: F.D. Marchetti. English Lyric: Dick Manning

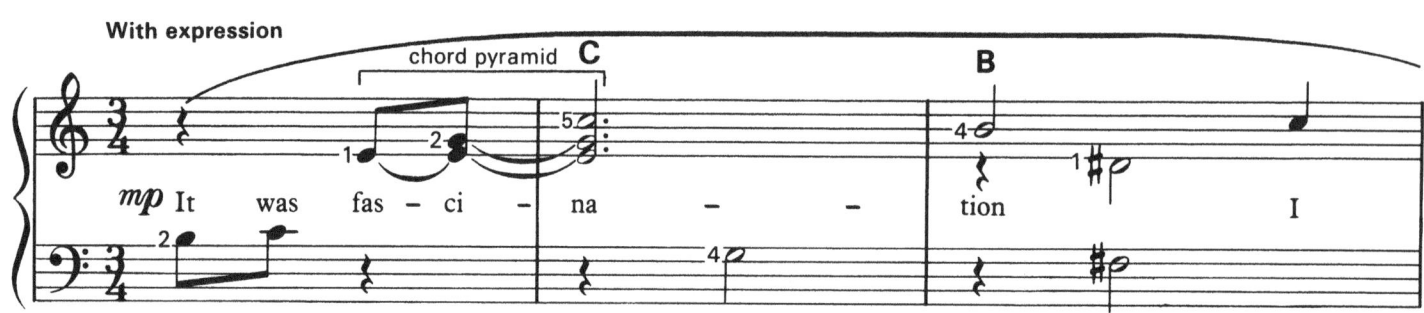

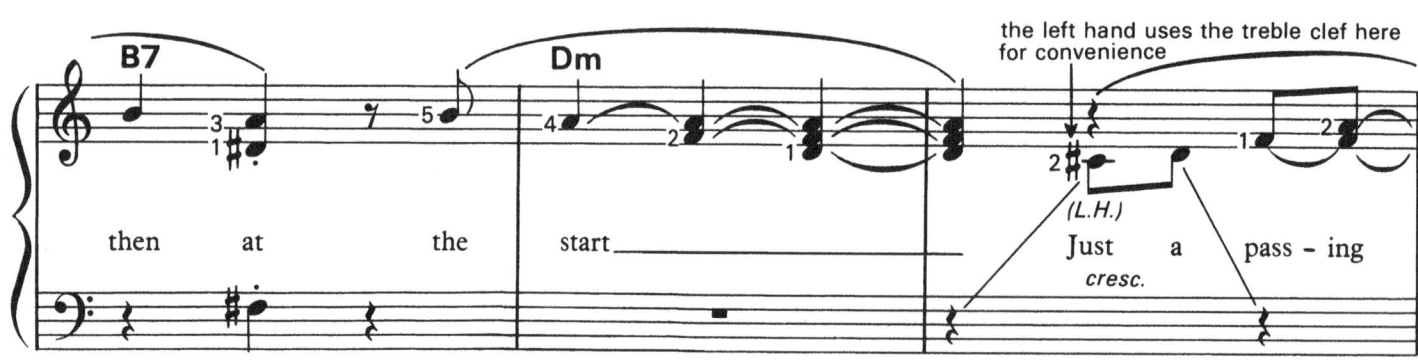

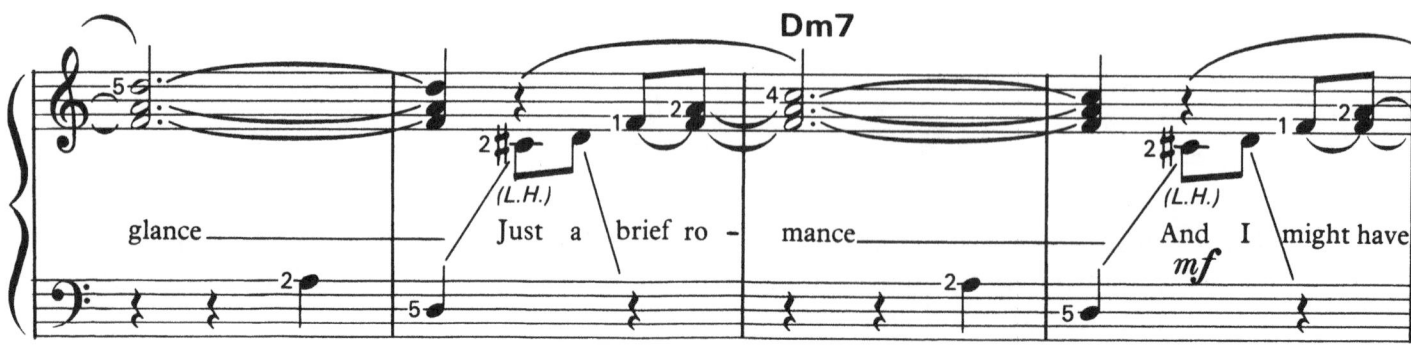

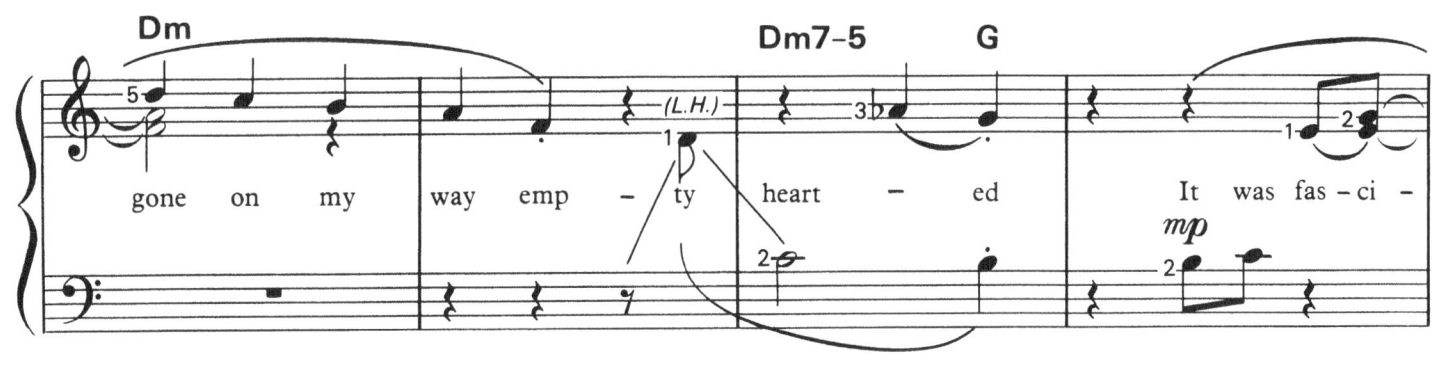
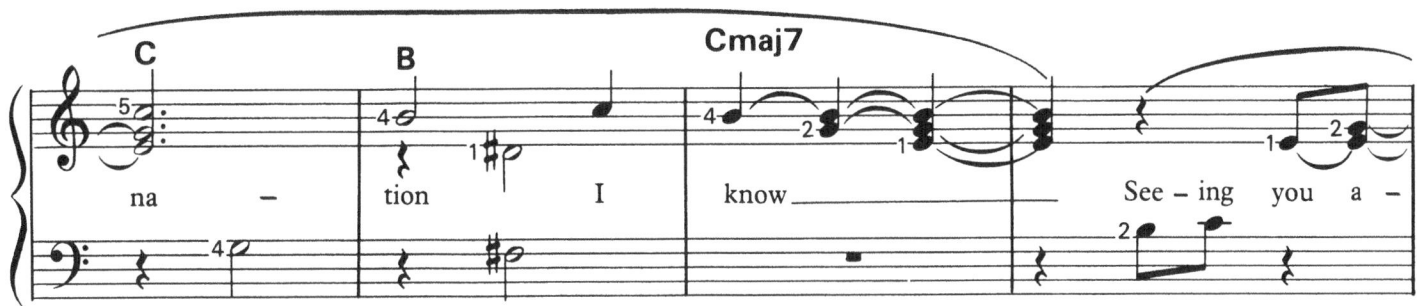
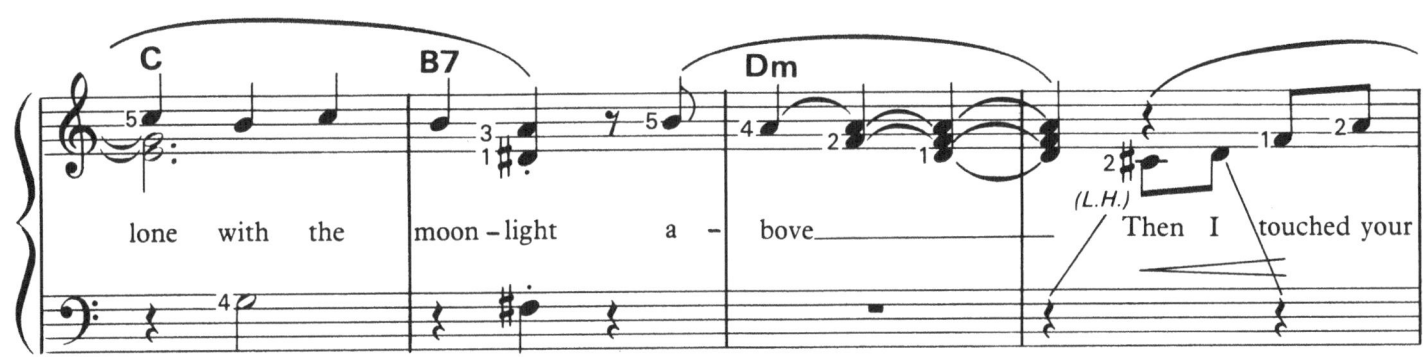
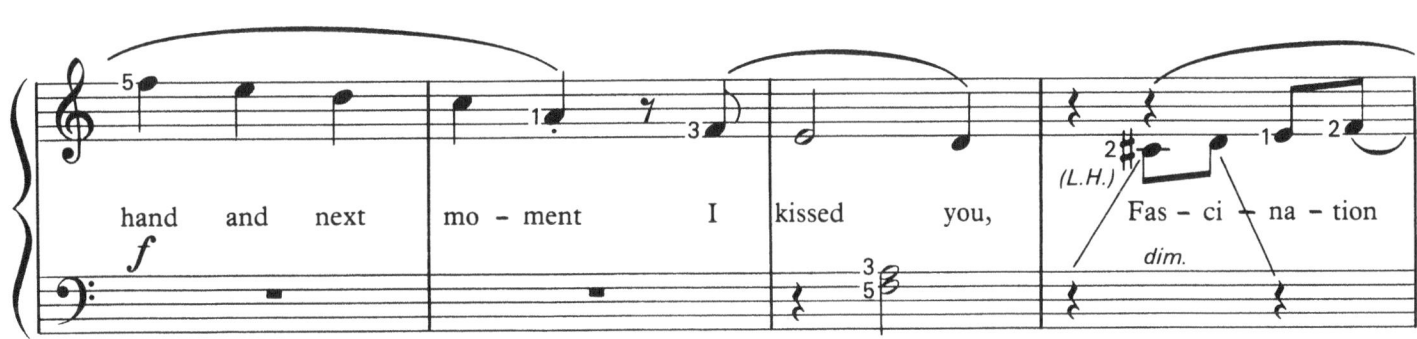
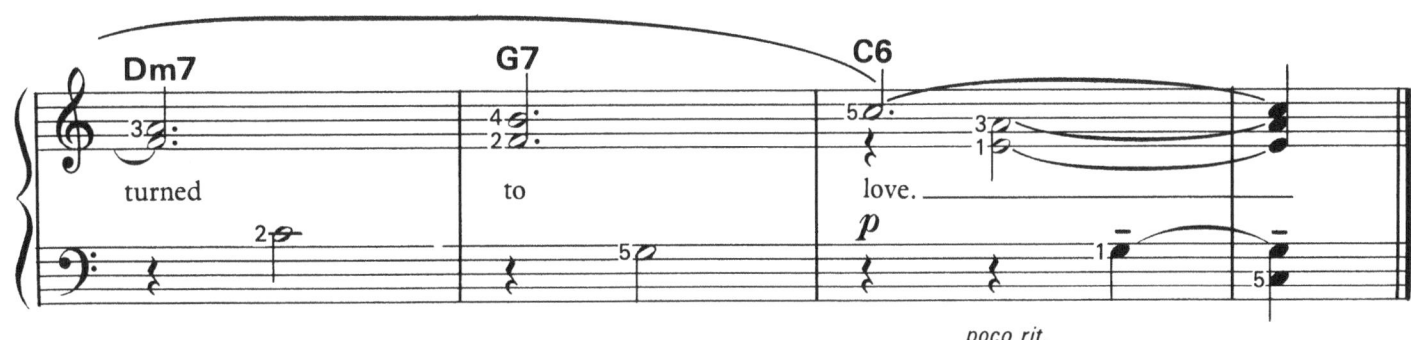

© Copyright 1904 F.D. Marchetti. © Copyright 1936 J. Liber.
© Copyright 1954 Liber-Southern Ltd. All rights reserved. International copyright secured.

poco rit.
(a little ritenuto: slowing down slightly)

NEW NOTES

2 Before tackling the next song, here are some new notes for you to learn:

G, A and low B for right hand
F, G, A and B for left hand

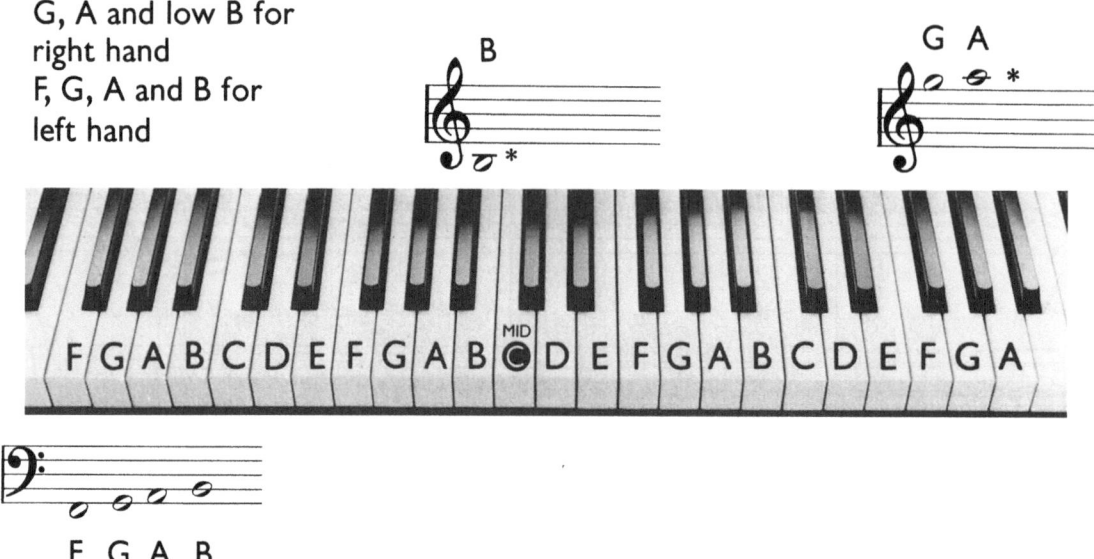

ACCOMPANIMENT PATTERNS

Notice the repeated accompaniment patterns in the left hand in *Spanish Eyes*.

SPANISH EYES
Words: Charles Singleton & Eddie Snyder. Music: Bert Kaempfert

*Ledger line: A partial line used to represent the full length line which would lie in that position (see Book One pages 15 and 16).

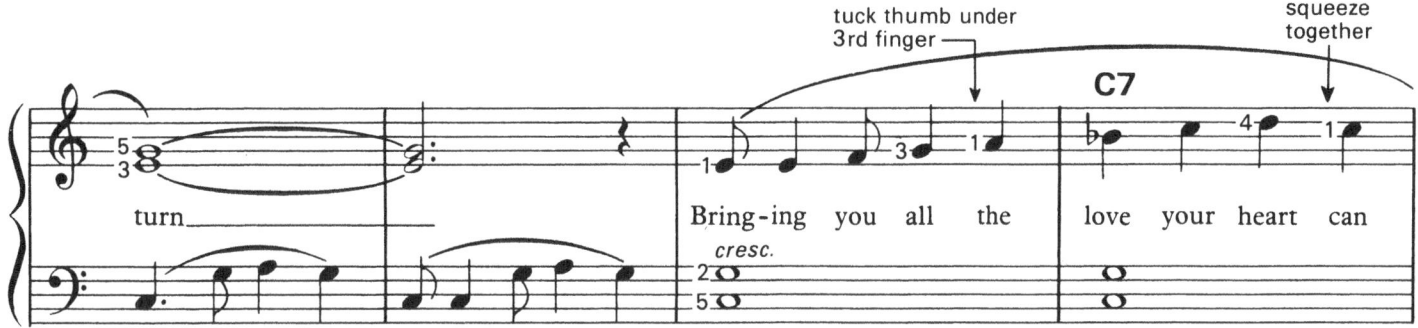

© Copyright 1965 Edition Doma Bert Kaempfert, Germany. Copyright for the World outside of Germany, Austria & Switzerland assigned to Roosevelt Music Co. Inc., USA. Carlin Music Corp., for the United Kingdom of Great Britain and Northern Ireland, Eire and the British Dominions, Colonies, Overseas Territories and Dependencies (exc. Canada, Australia and New Zealand). All rights reserved. International copyright secured.

PHRASES AND PHRASING

A 'phrase' is a group of notes which belong together musically.
'Phrasing' refers to the way in which the notes are played.
Usually you play the notes of your phrases legato (joined up):

SMILE (Book 3, p.6)

a legato phrase

Sometimes you play them staccato (disconnected):

Theme from WILLIAM TELL OVERTURE (Book 2, p.44)

a staccato phrase

In "Dream Baby", you will be using a mixture of staccato and legato phrasing. You will also be accenting certain notes. Such different types of phrasing within a piece help to give it contrast, and contrast is one of the most important aspects of phrasing.

Note the repeated accompaniment 'patterns' in the left hand of "Dream Baby".

DREAM BABY
(HOW LONG MUST I DREAM)

Words & Music: Cindy Walker

KEY OF G

4

The key of G (Major) is derived from the scale of G (Major), which requires one black note: F sharp:

Scale of G

G A B C D E (F#) G

Pieces using this scale predominantly are said to be in the key of G.
The key signature for the key of G is:

Key of G

F sharp
F sharp

When you are in this key you must remember to play every F (wherever it might fall on the keyboard) as F sharp.

BLUE MOON
Words: Lorenz Hart. Music: Richard Rodgers

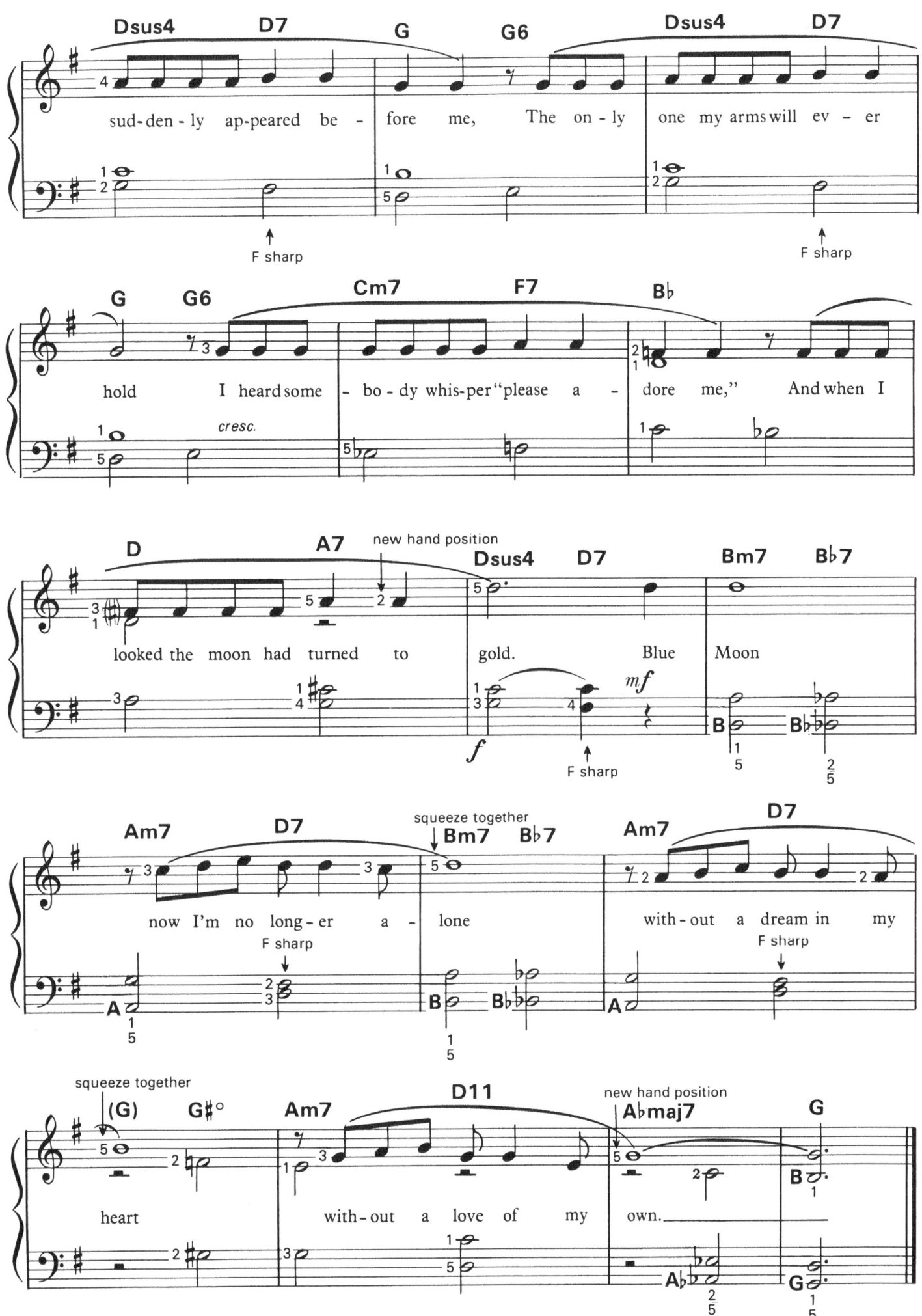

6/8 TIME

5

This means six quavers (six "eighth" notes), or their equivalent, per bar.

In 6/8 time the dotted crotchet (dotted quarter note) ♩. is the basic beat, and there are two dotted crotchets per bar:

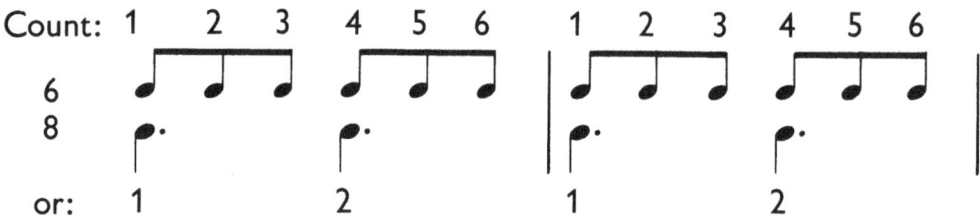

The player may count either 6 quavers or 2 dotted crotchets per bar, whichever is more convenient.

In slow pieces e.g. *Greensleeves* (p.17) it will probably be more convenient to count 6 in a bar:

GREENSLEEVES

In faster pieces e.g. *Liberty Bell* (p.20) it will probably be better to count 2 in a bar:

LIBERTY BELL

GREENSLEEVES
Traditional

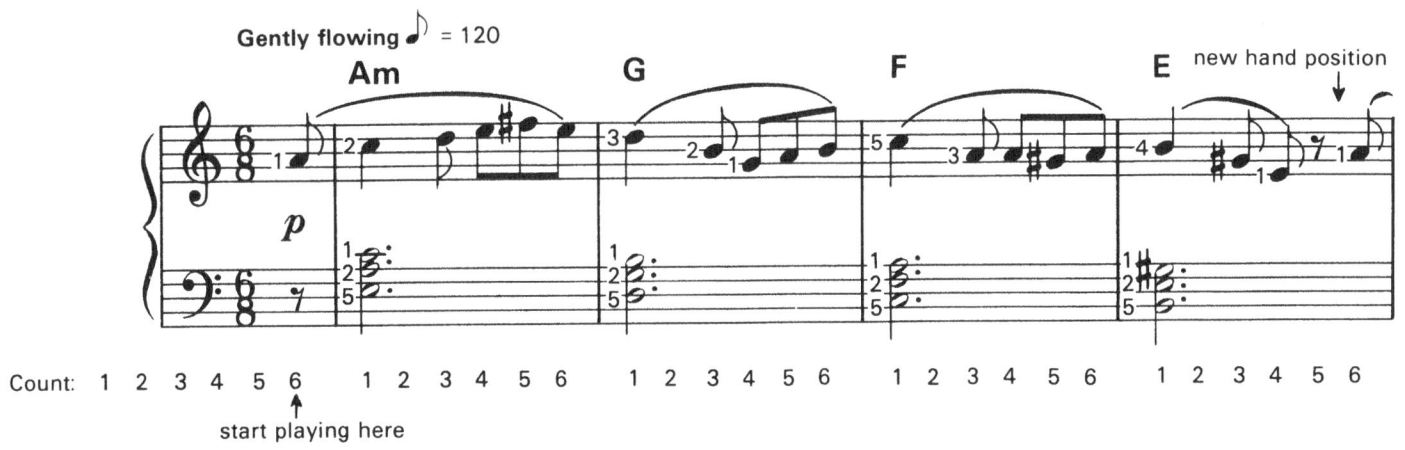

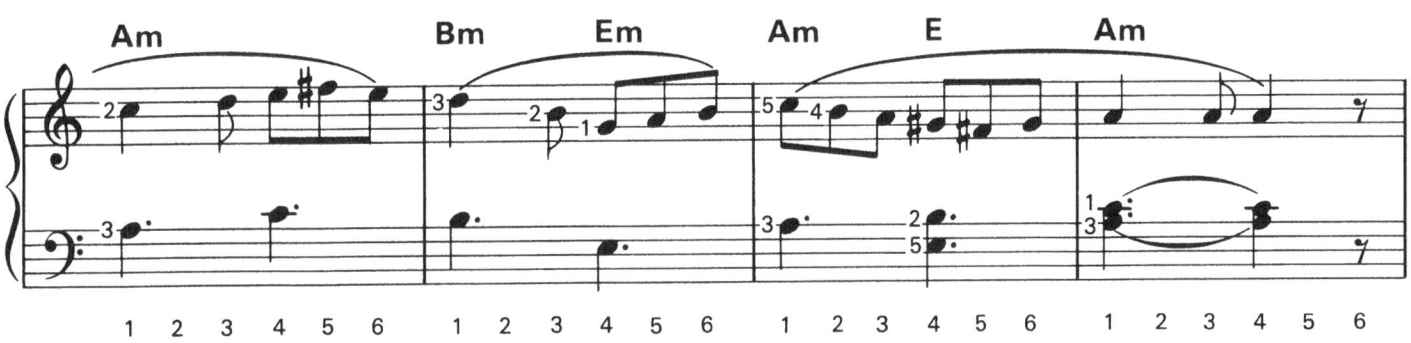

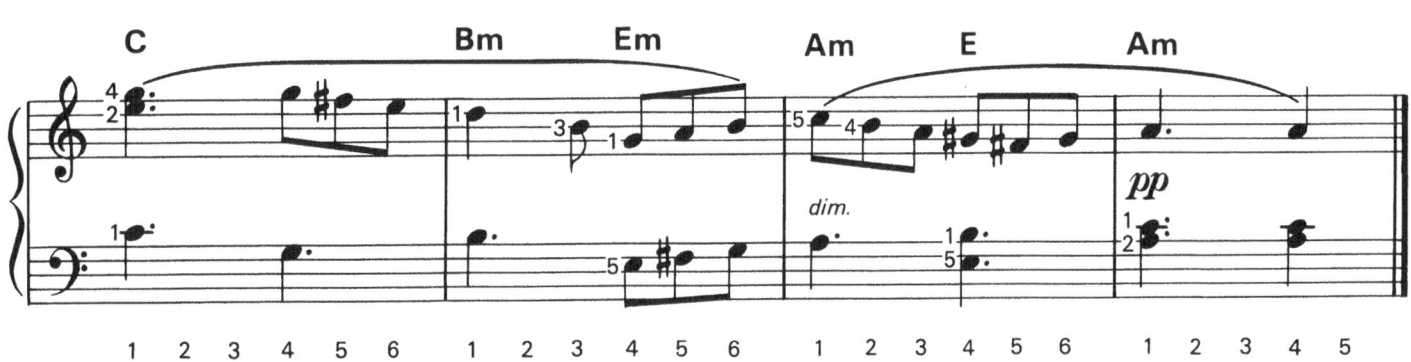

© Copyright 1984 by Dorsey Brothers Music Ltd. All rights reserved. International copyright secured.

THE TWO-NOTE SLUR

6

You learnt in Book One (p.36) that a slur, sometimes called a phrase mark, is a curved line covering the notes, indicating that they are to be played legato:

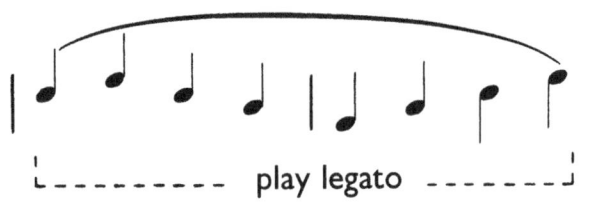

When a slur covers two notes only:

stress the first note (play slightly louder); let the second note be weak (play softer and staccato).

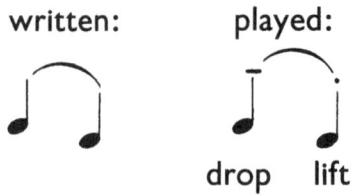

Let your hand *drop* onto the first note and *lift* up from the second note. This will give you the correct sound of the two-note slur.

I have arrowed the two-note slurs in the following piece.

NORWEGIAN WOOD
Words & Music: John Lennon and Paul McCartney

NEW NOTE

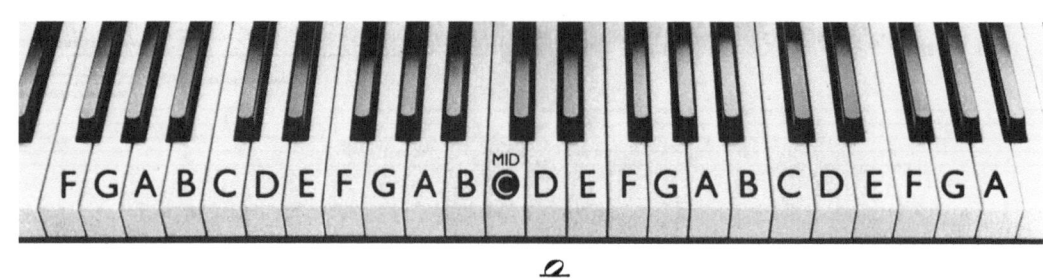

High D for left hand

Look for the new D note in the following three pieces.

LIBERTY BELL
By J.P. Sousa

*March tempo ♩. = 92

*A piece of music with a strongly emphasised regular metre.

ARPEGGIO (BROKEN CHORD) STYLE FOR LEFT HAND

8

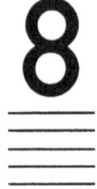

This is another useful accompaniment style, similar in effect to strumming chords on a guitar or banjo.
It is indicated by means of a wavy line:

A SUMMER PLACE

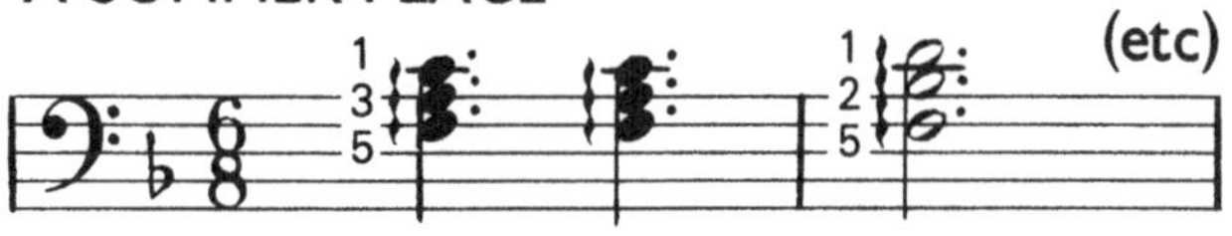

Play the notes of the chord(s) in rapid succession upwards, rolling your wrist from left to right, yet keeping the wrist relaxed.
Sustain each note on the way up in order to get a rich, full sound.

(THEME FROM) A SUMMER PLACE

By Max Steiner

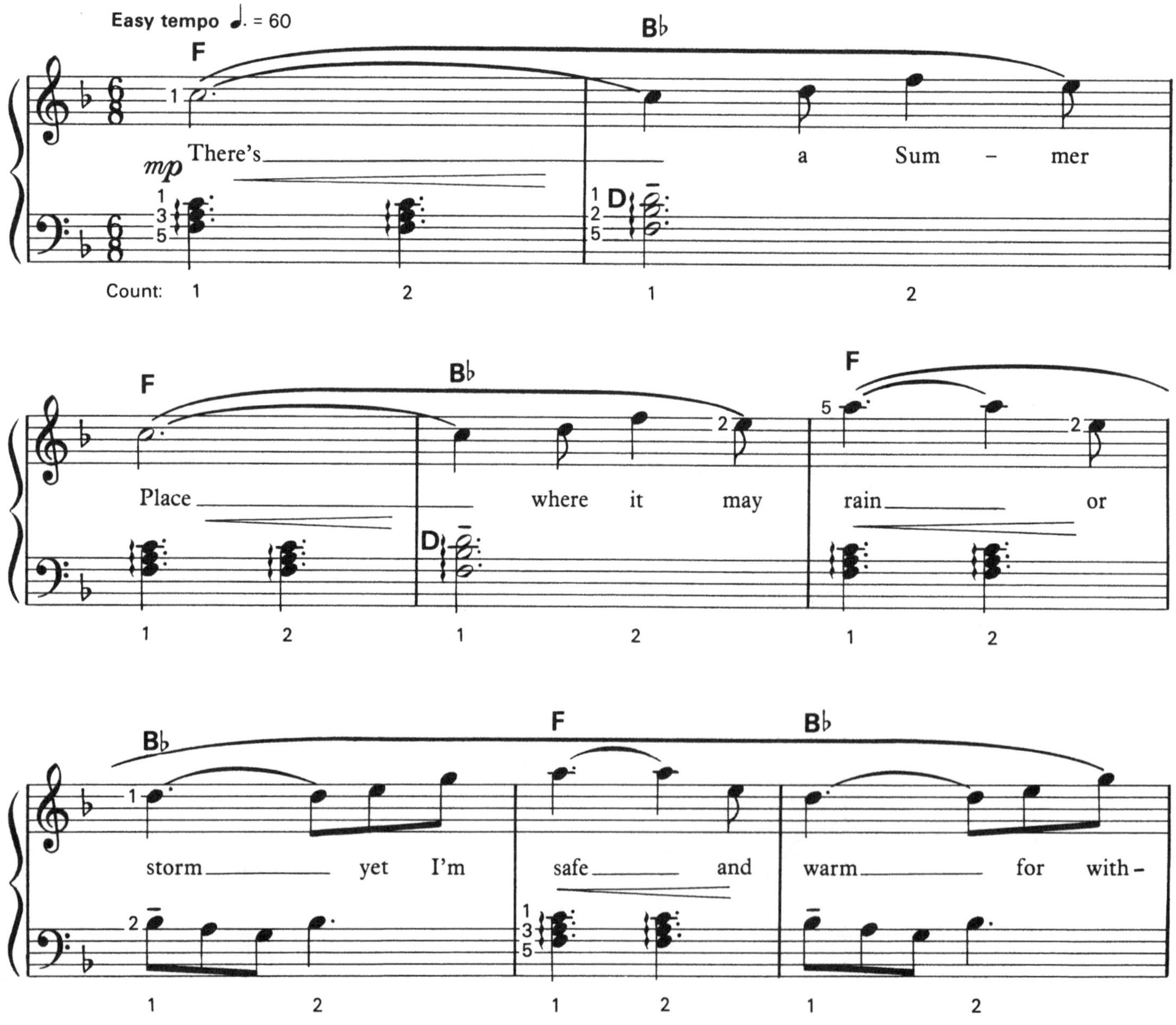

© Copyright 1960 by M. Witmark & Sons, USA. Warner Bros Music Ltd., for the British Commonwealth of Nations (exc. Canada & Australasia) and Eire.
All rights reserved. International copyright secured.

SEMIQUAVERS (SIXTEENTH NOTES)

9

Written:

Semiquavers move twice as fast as quavers:

Semiquavers are featured in the next piece, *Morning*, by Grieg. To get the basic timing, start by counting the piece in 6:

MORNING

Count: 1 2 3 4 5 6   1 2 3 4 5 and 6 and
(Later): 1   2   1   2

Later on you will find that the piece will flow better if you count in 2.

MORNING from 'Peer Gynt'
By Edvard Grieg

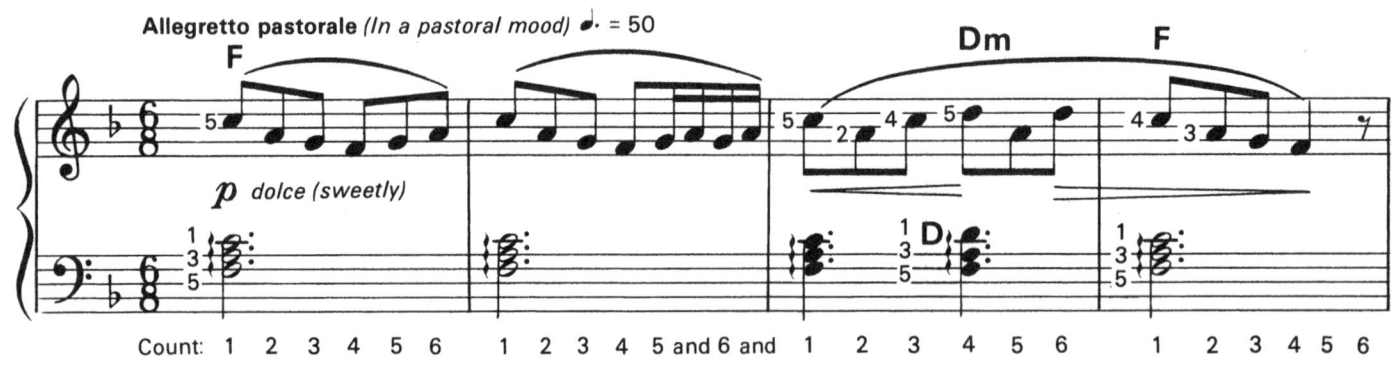

THE WALTZ

Although waltzes vary in speed, they are always written in 3/4 time.

In *Somewhere My Love* (Lara's Theme, from Doctor Zhivago) observe the two-note slurs in the left hand. These will help give the piece "lift".

SOMEWHERE MY LOVE (LARA'S THEME)
Words: Paul Francis Webster. Music: Maurice Jarre

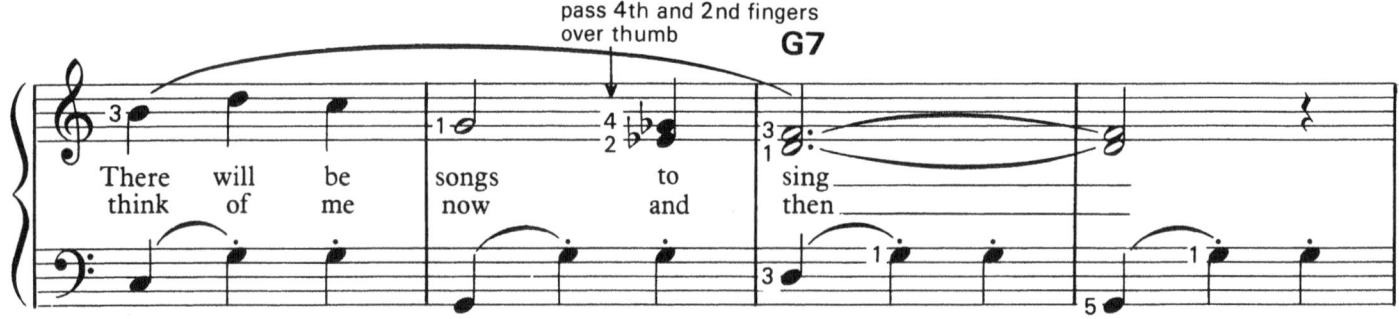

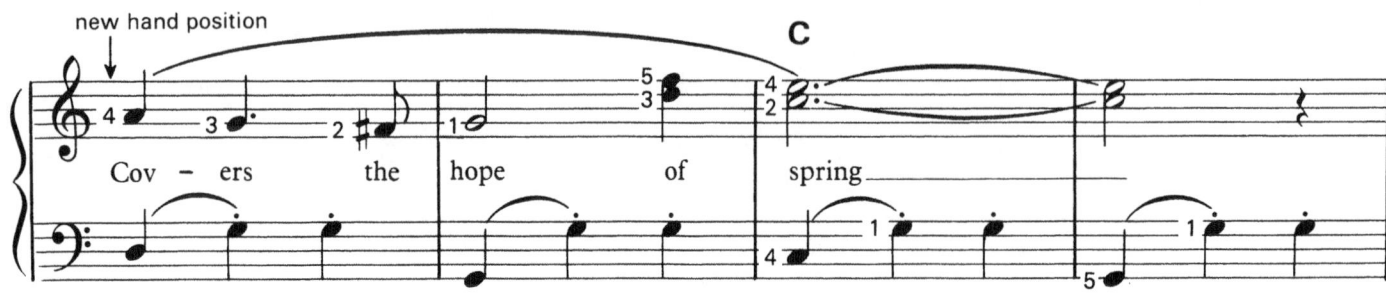

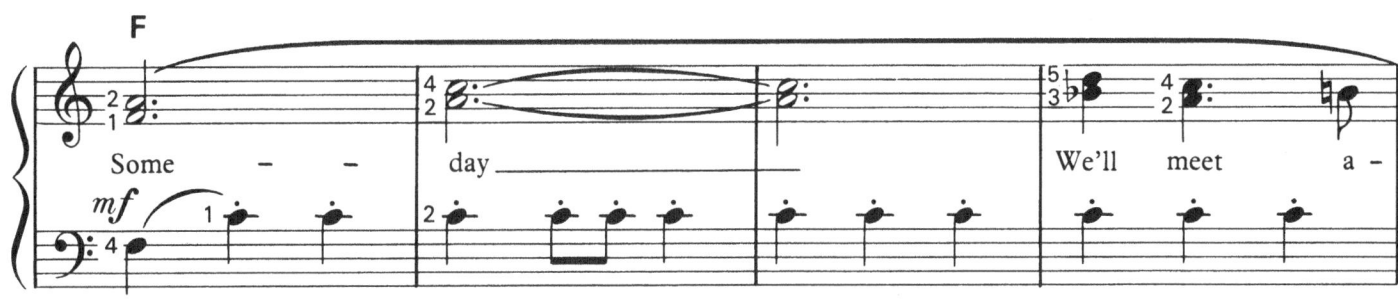
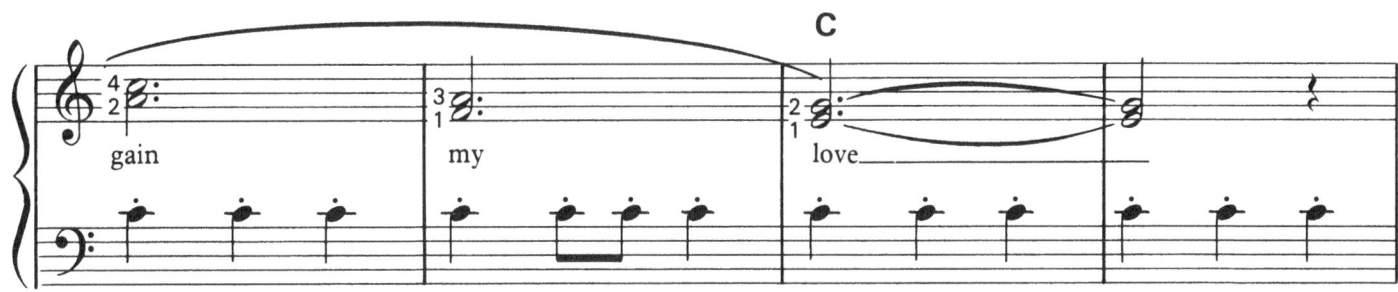

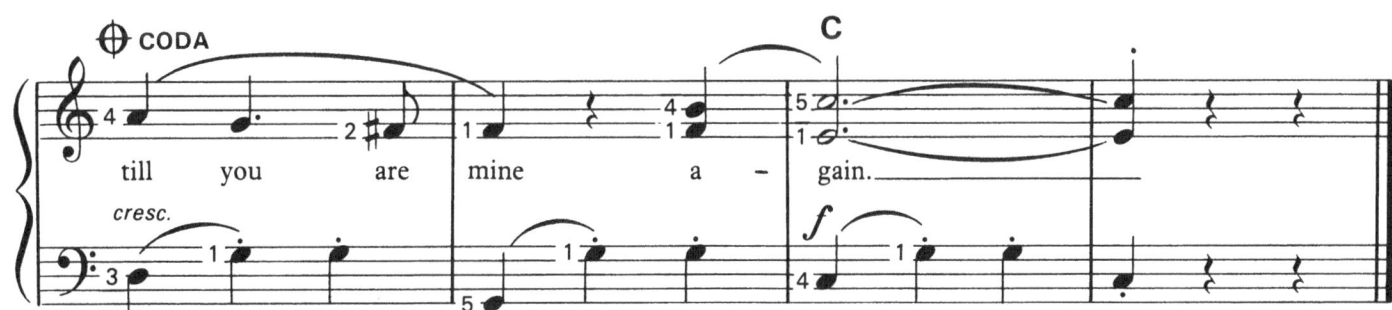

***Da Capo Al Coda:** From the beginning to Coda.
Repeat from the beginning of the piece until **to Coda** ⊕
From there jump to the **Coda** (the final section of the piece) and play through to the end.

© Copyright 1965 & 1966 MGM Inc., USA. Rights throughout the world controlled by Robbins Music Corp, USA.
Administered by Big Three Music Ltd., for the UK & Eire. All rights reserved. International copyright secured.

GRACE NOTES

Grace notes are ornamental notes not included in the basic timing of the bar. They are always written small:

OB LA DI, OB LA DA

Play your grace notes as quickly as possible. So, in the above example, hold your minim C for almost its full length. Then slip in the two grace notes just before the crotchet F, which is due on beat 1 of the next bar.

OB-LA-DI, OB-LA-DA
Words & Music: John Lennon and Paul McCartney

*A strong accent.

***Acciaccatura.** A type of grace note. Play the acciaccatura note as quickly as possible.

© Copyright 1968 Northern Songs Limited. All rights reserved. International copyright secured.

ACCIDENTALS

Accidentals are sharps, flats, or naturals which are not expected, because they are not included in the key signature. In the following piece, *Over The Rainbow*, only the F sharp is expected (key of G). All other sharps and flats, and the rather frequent F naturals, are accidentals.

Remember that accidentals only apply to the bar in which they occur. At the next bar everything returns to normal.

OVER THE RAINBOW
Words: E.Y. Harburg. Music: Harold Arlen

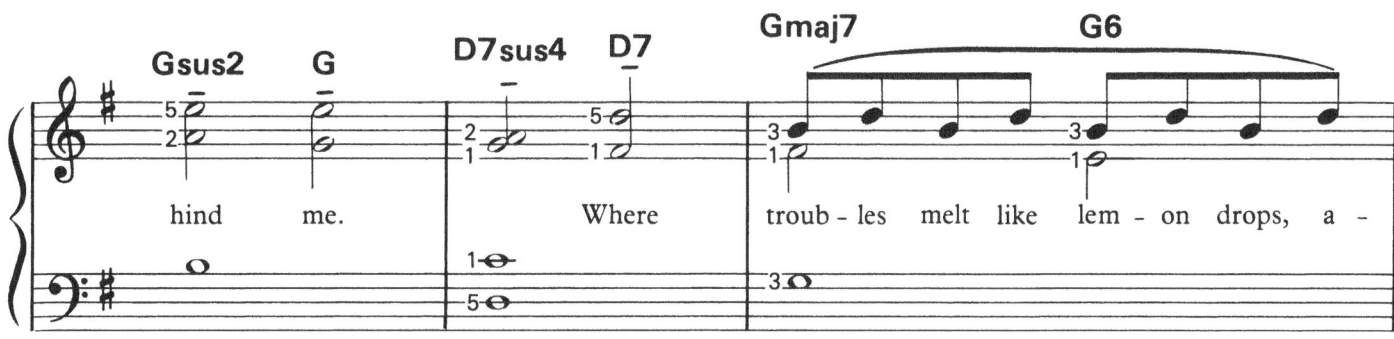

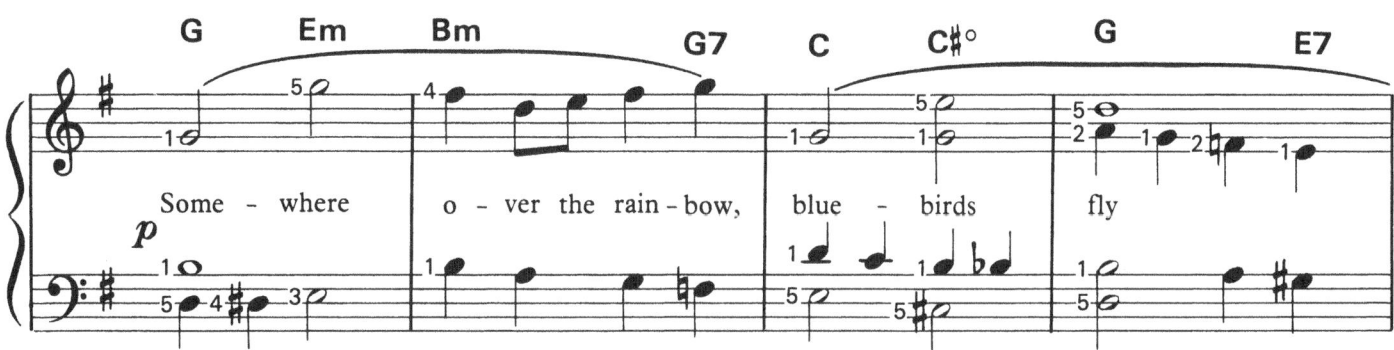
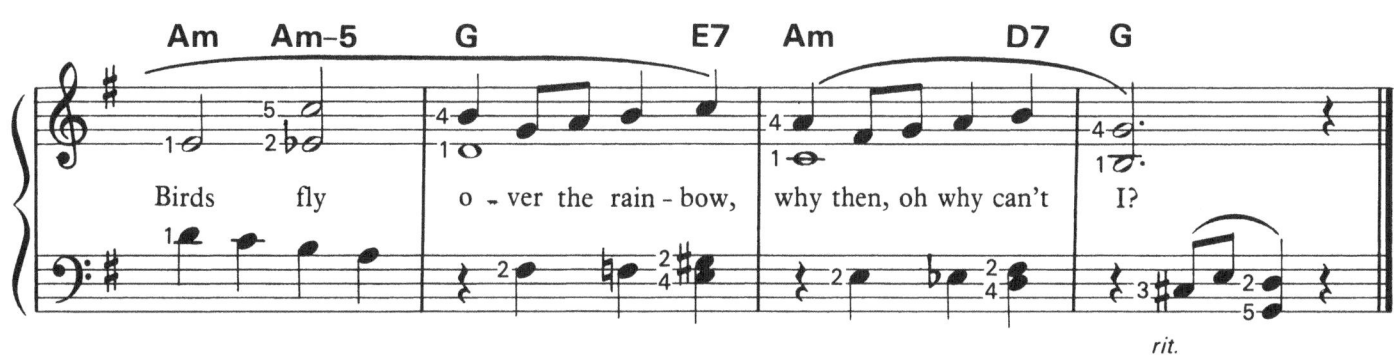

© Copyright 1938 (renewed 1966) by MGM Inc., USA. © Copyright 1939 (renewed 1967) by Leo Feist Inc., USA. Rights throughout the world controlled by Leo Feist Inc., USA. Administered by Big Three Music Ltd., for the UK & Eire. All rights reserved. International copyright secured.

REPEATED NOTES

On a number of occasions in your next piece, *Irish Washerwoman*, a note has to be repeated i.e. struck rapidly twice in succession:

IRISH WASHERWOMAN

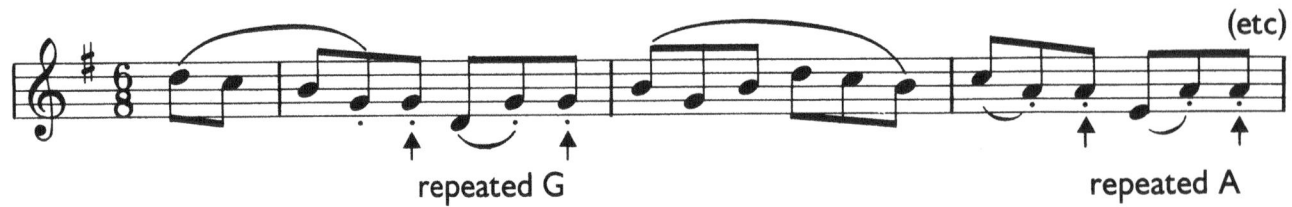

Be sure to play the first of each pair of repeated notes staccato, otherwise the note will not be ready for use again. You will find 'slur' phrasing, with the hand doing a drop-lift movement each time, a great help in these repeated note passages.

IRISH WASHERWOMAN
Traditional

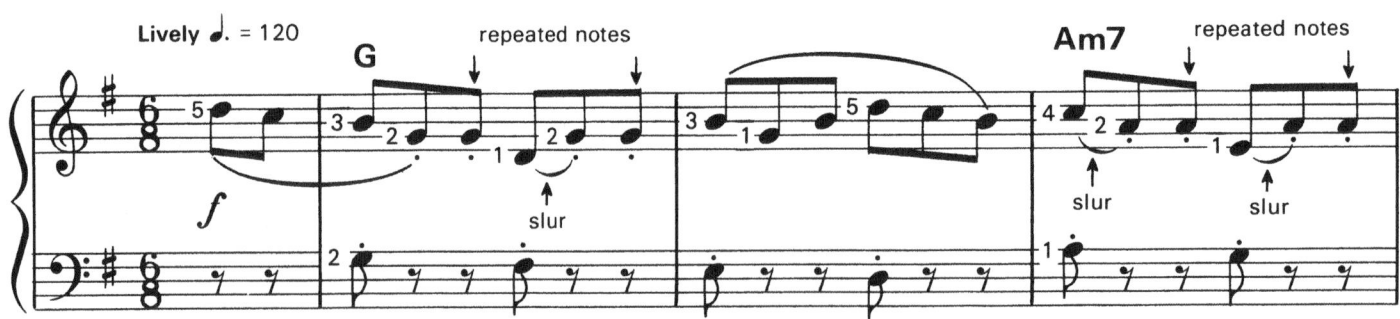

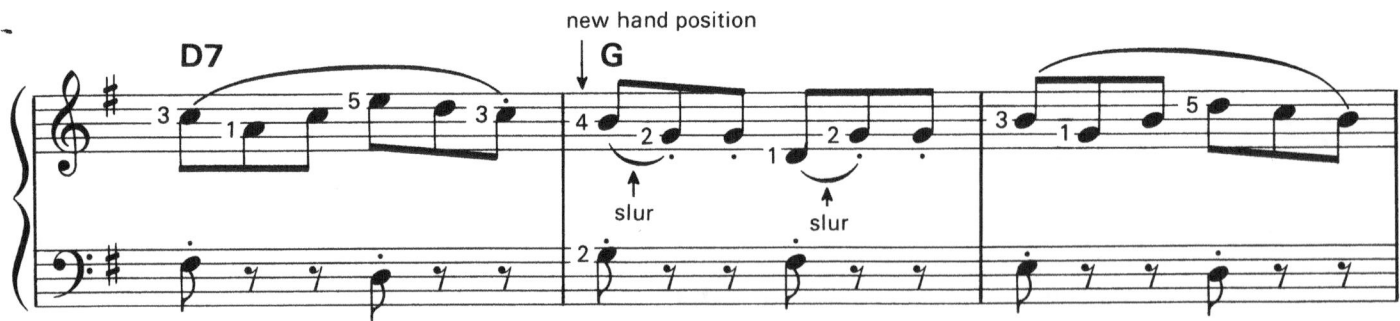

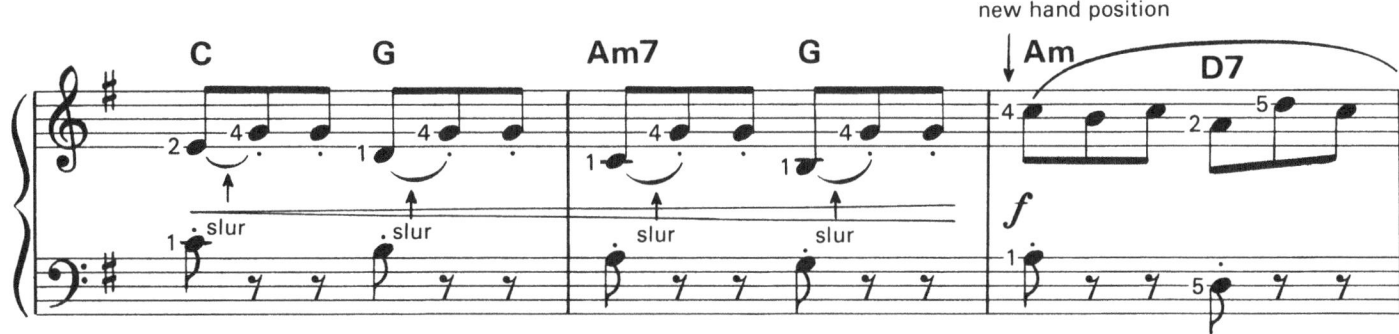

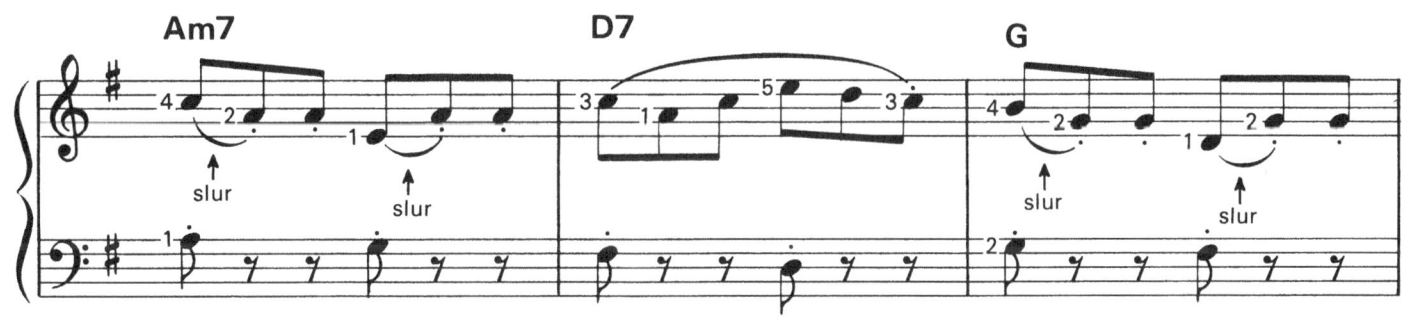

© Copyright 1984 Dorsey Brothers Music Ltd. All rights reserved. International copyright secured.

SEMIQUAVERS (SIXTEENTH NOTES) IN $\frac{4}{4}$ TIME

14

In the next piece, *Imagine,* which is written in Common Time($\frac{4}{4}$) there are a number of semiquaver (sixteenth note) fragments mixed in with quavers, crotchets, and other time notes.

In such a situation it is probably best, at least in the early stages, to count in quavers rather than crotchets. Each semiquaver will then have a recognisable place in the count:

At a later stage, when you have the feel of the timing, you could try counting 4 crotchets to the bar, rather than 8 quavers:

IMAGINE

Words & Music: John Lennon

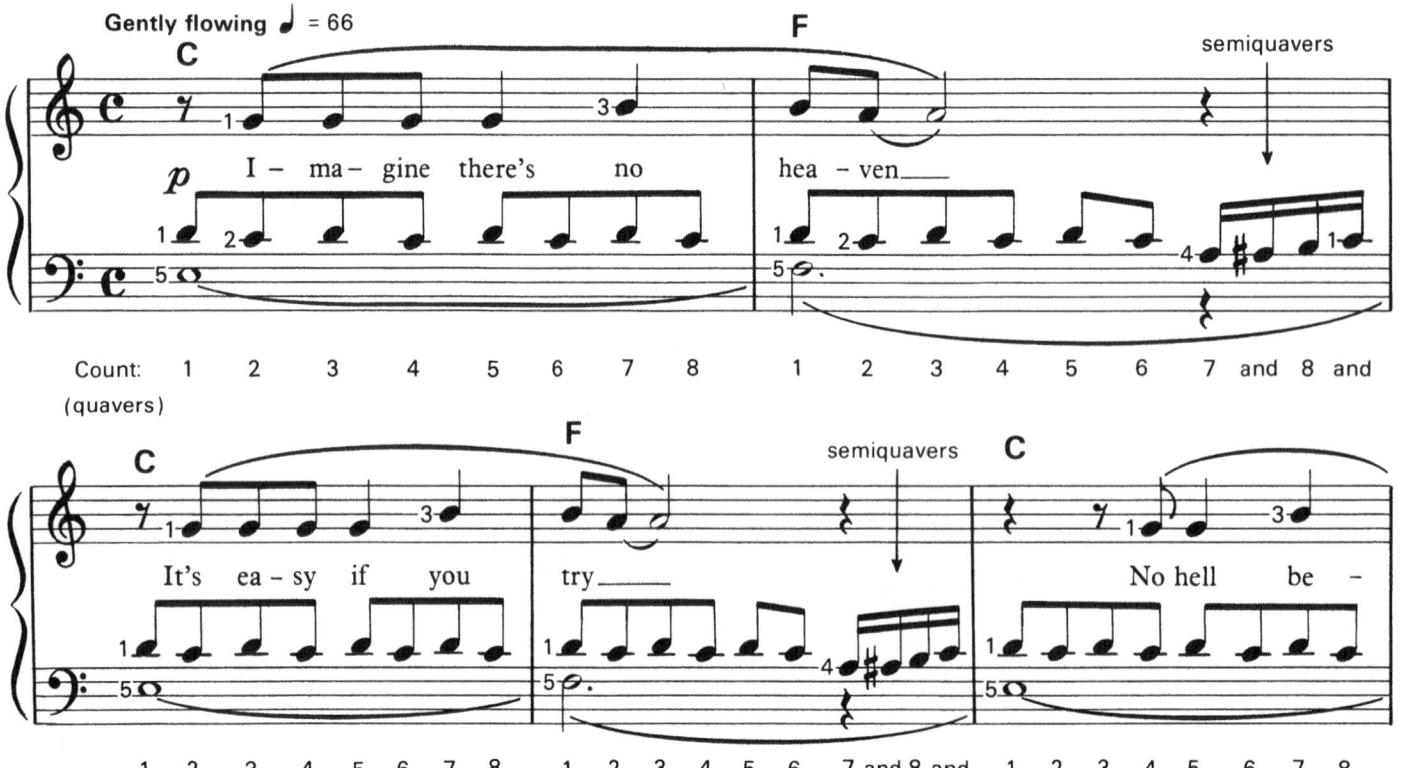

34

NEW NOTES

B, C for right hand
High E for left hand

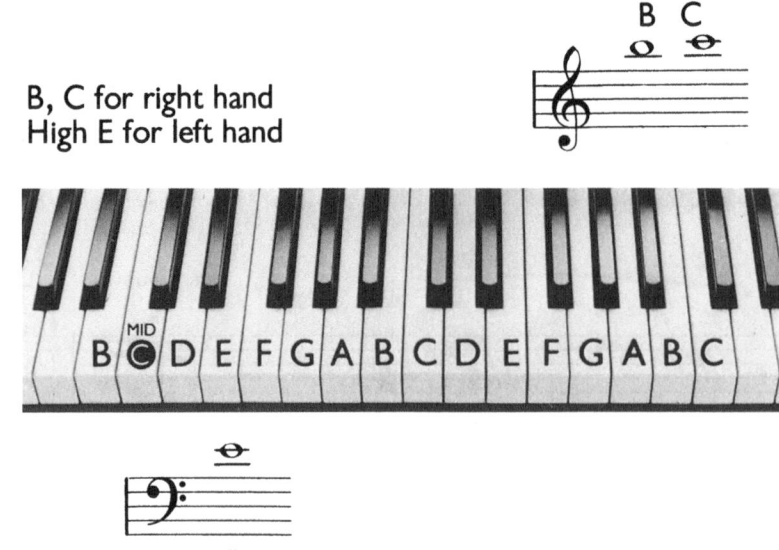

Watch out for these new notes in the next few pieces, the first of which is a charming little piano piece from the Anna Magdalena Notebooks by Bach.

MINUET IN G
By Johann Sebastian Bach

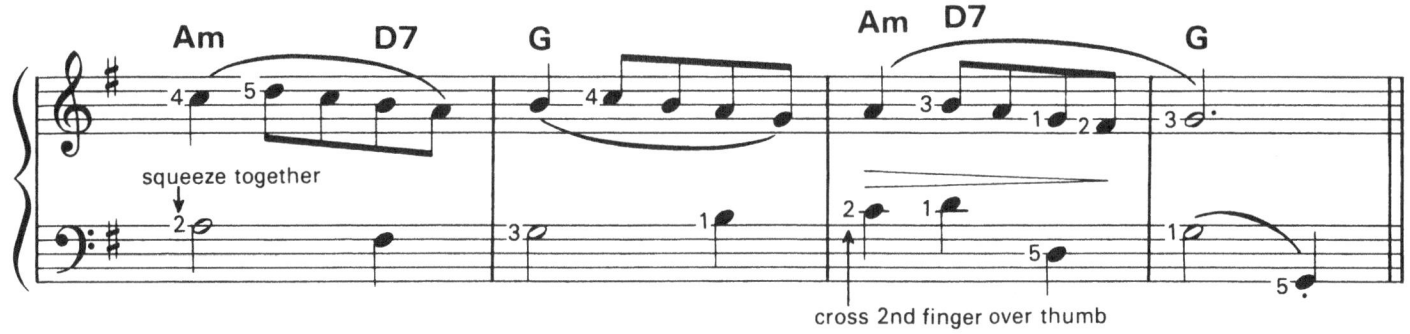
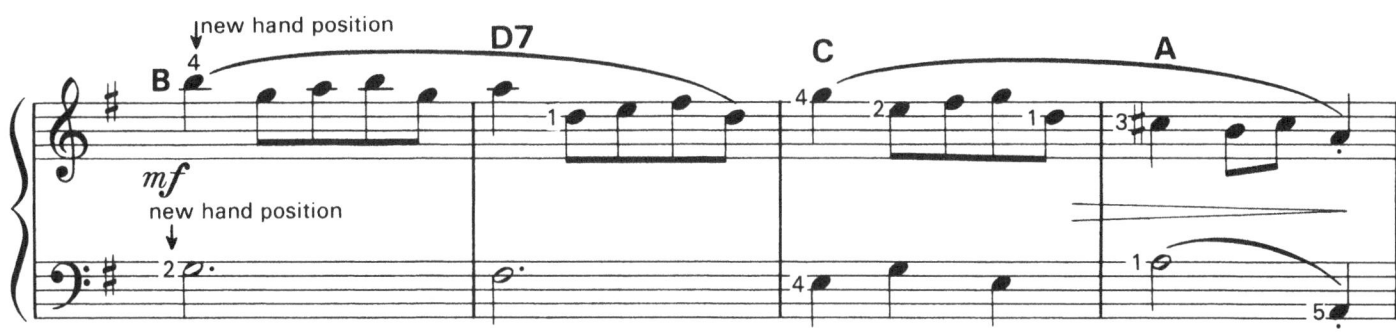
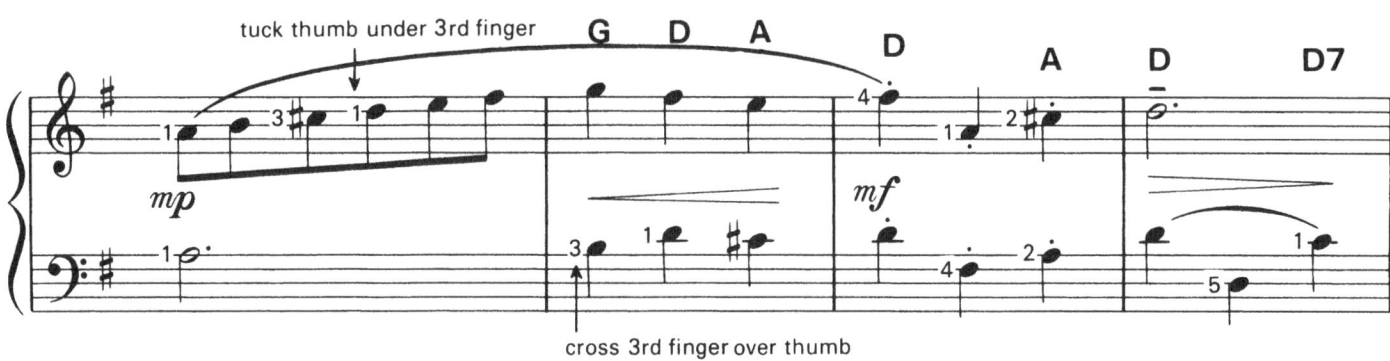
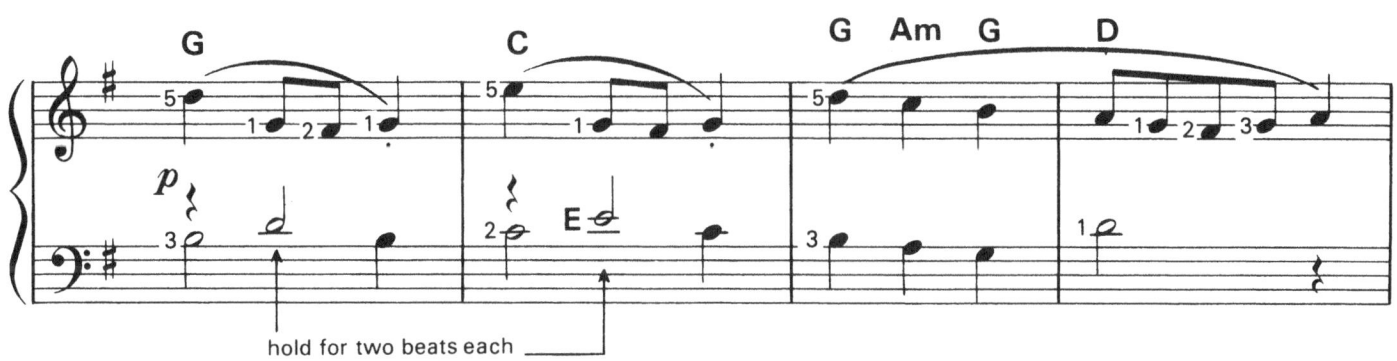
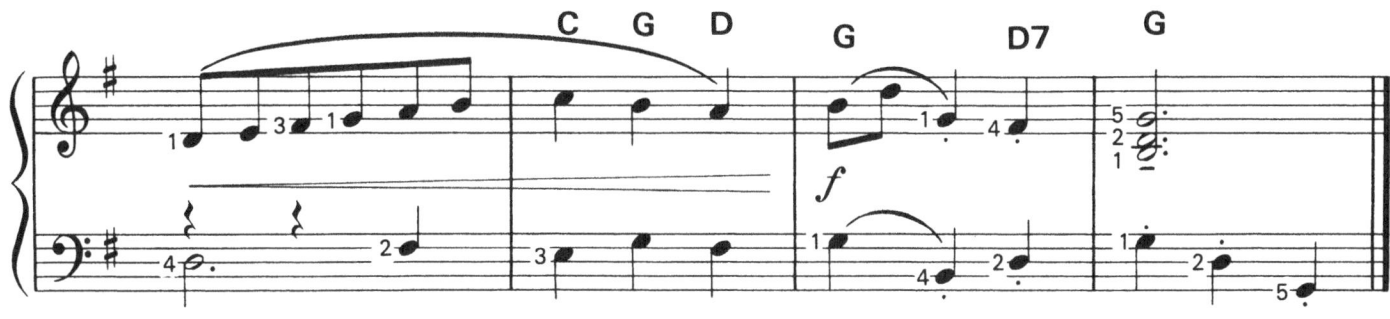

© Copyright 1984 Dorsey Brothers Music Ltd. All rights reserved. International copyright secured.

TRIPLETS

A triplet is a group of 3 notes played in the time of 2.

The most common type of triplet – the quaver triplet – is written like this:

quaver (eighth note) triplet

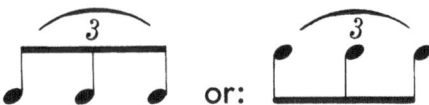

Compare the counting of normal quavers and triplet quavers:

normal quavers

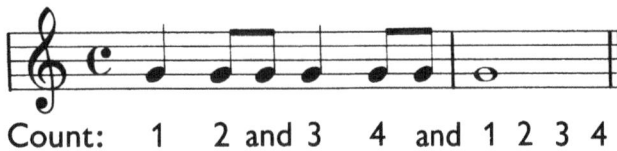

Count: 1   2 and 3   4 and 1 2 3 4

triplet quavers

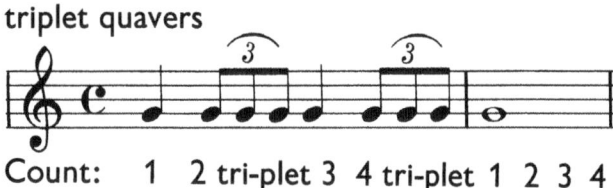

Count: 1   2 tri-plet 3   4 tri-plet 1 2 3 4

You will note that the triplet quavers move slightly faster than the normal quavers – they have to in order to fit the bar. Be sure to keep your triplet notes regular and even.

Quaver triplets appear in your next piece, *Amazing Grace*.

ARPEGGIO (BROKEN CHORD) STYLE FOR BOTH HANDS

In *Amazing Grace* arpeggios work their way upwards through both hands. Start with the lowest left hand note and play rapidly upwards, sustaining each note as you go.

AMAZING GRACE
Traditional

CROTCHET (QUARTER NOTE) TRIPLET

17

This is another common type of triplet. It consists of 3 crotchets (quarter notes) played in the time of 2:

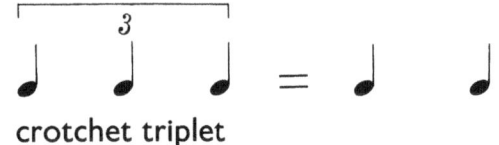
crotchet triplet

Compare the counting of normal crotchets and triplet crotchets:

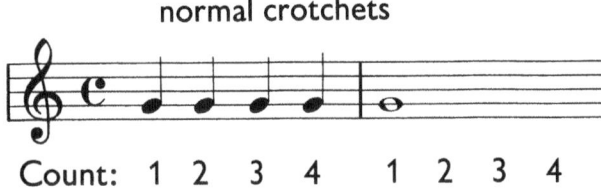

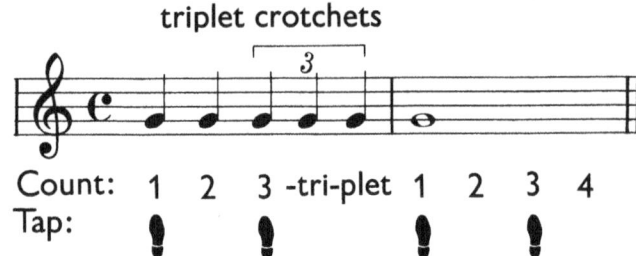

Tap your foot on beats 1 and 3. Start your triplet on beat 3 (a foot-tap) and be ready to play the semibreve G on beat 1 of the next bar (the next foot tap). Make sure that your triplet notes in between are regular and even.

The next piece, the theme from the film *Lawrence Of Arabia* will give you plenty of practice in both crotchet and quaver triplets.

LAWRENCE OF ARABIA
By Maurice Jarre

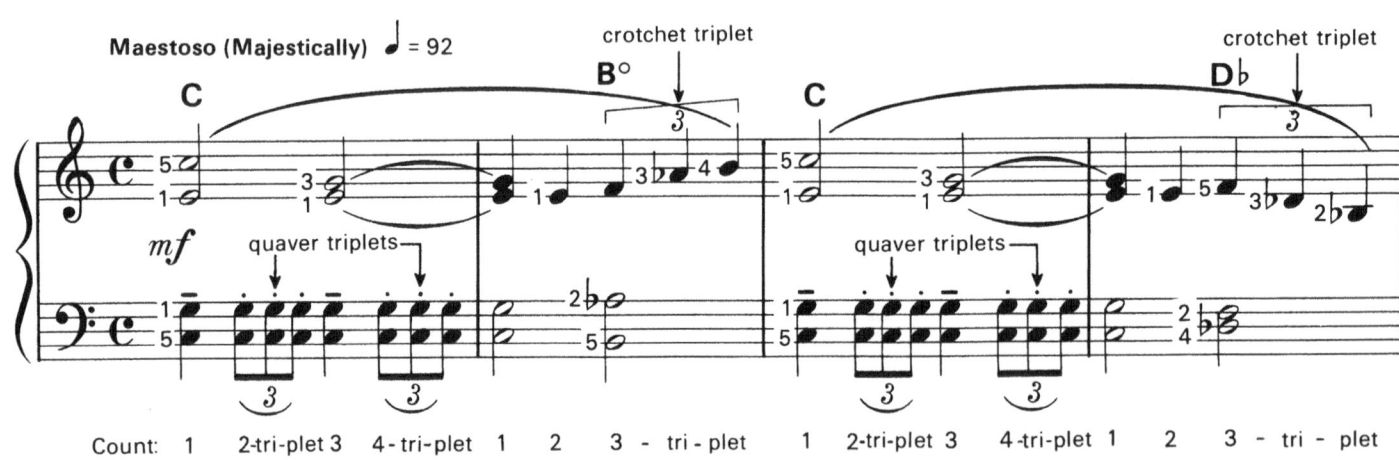

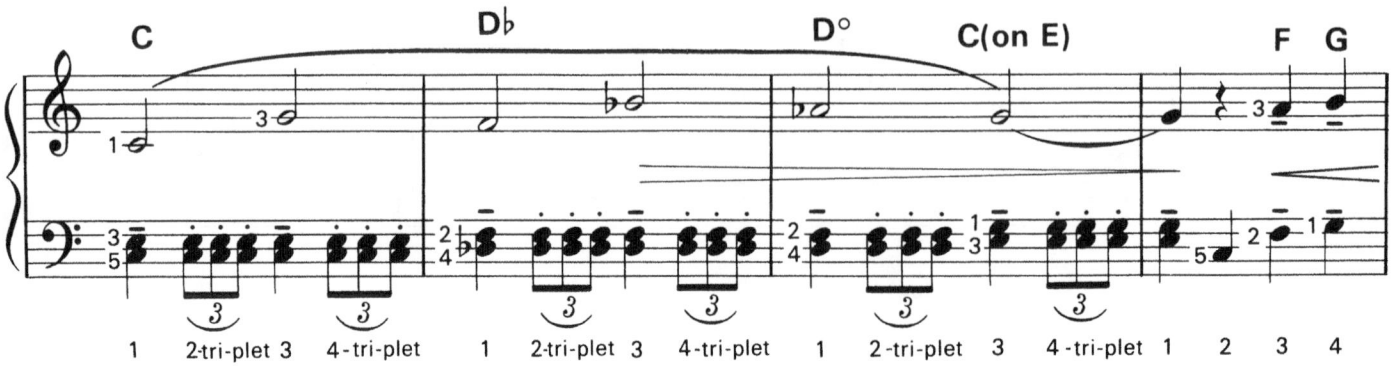

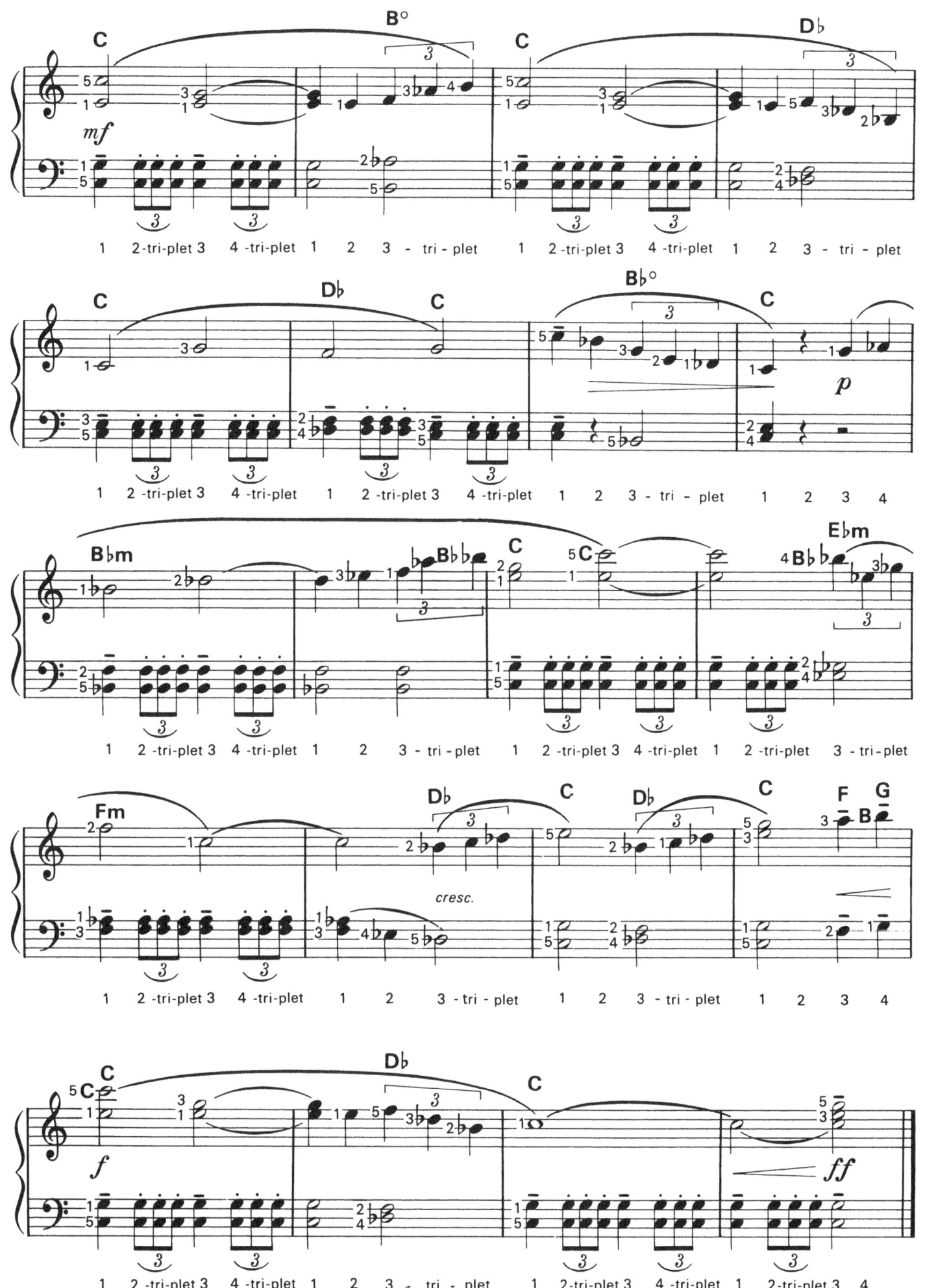

MORE LEFT HAND MELODY PLAYING

For much of the next piece, "I'm Not In Love", the melody is in the left hand part. Play your right hand chords rhythmically, but keep them well in the background so that your left hand melody can sing through.

I'M NOT IN LOVE

Words & Music: Eric Stewart & Graham Gouldman

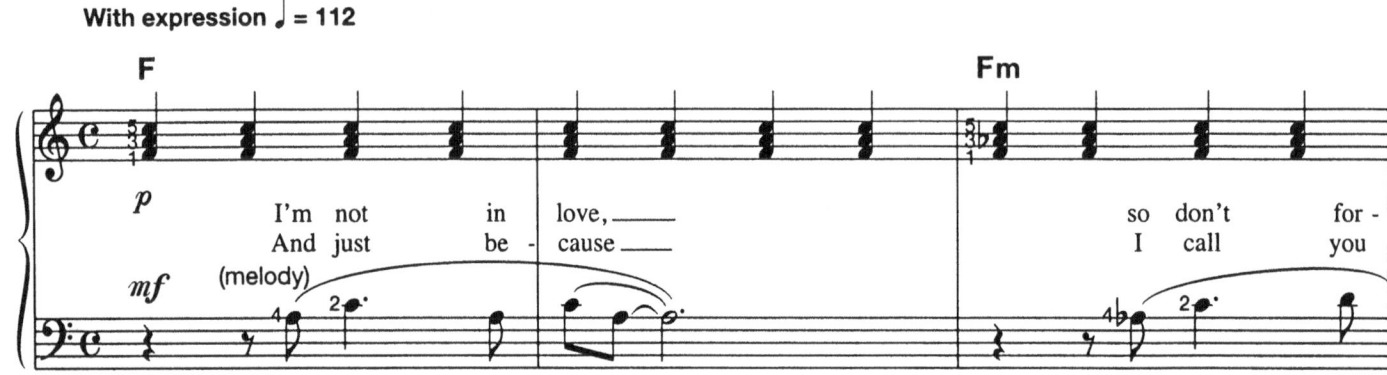

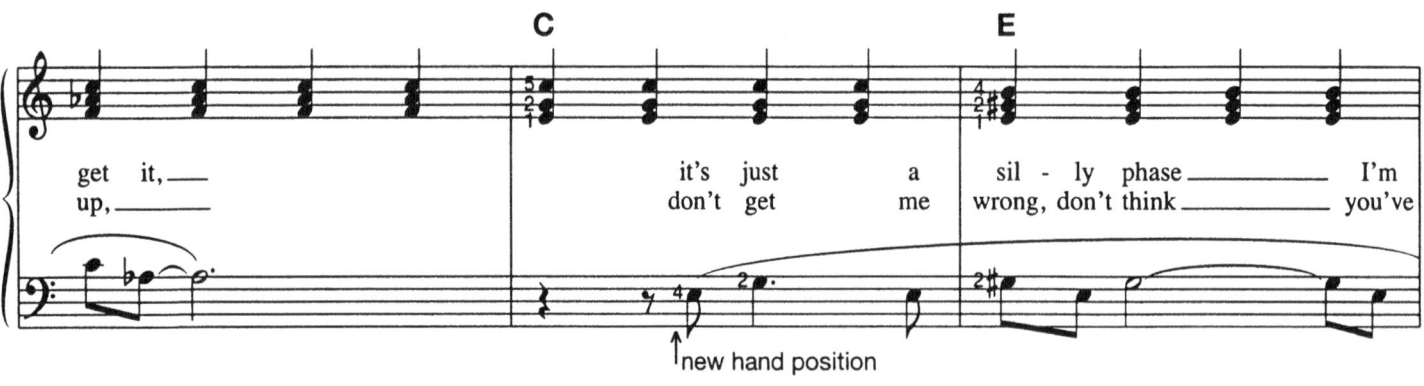

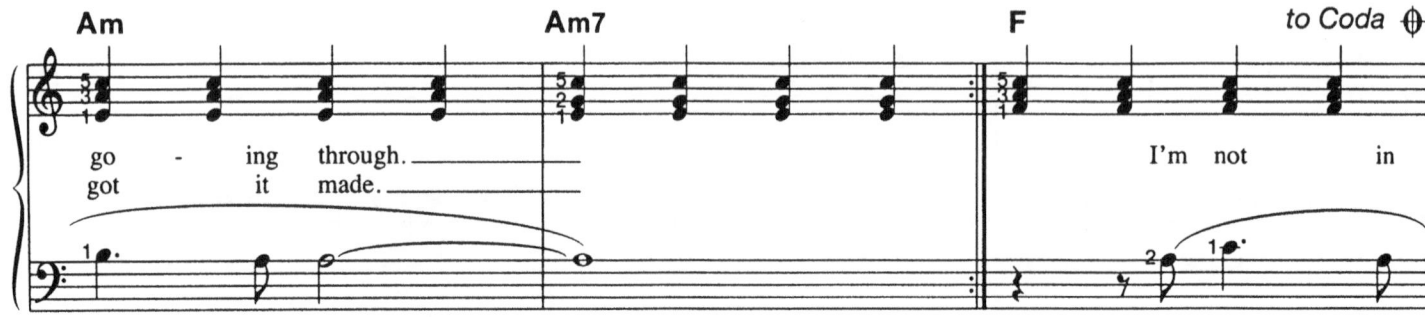

THE DOTTED QUAVER (DOTTED EIGHTH NOTE)

As you learnt in Book Two, (p.38), a dot after a note increases its length by one-half. So, a dotted quaver (dotted eighth note) is equal to 1½ quavers, or 3 semiquavers:

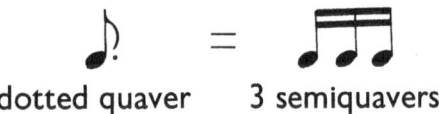

dotted quaver   3 semiquavers

A dotted quaver (dotted eighth) rest, a silence equal to one dotted quaver, is written like this:

𝟽·   dotted quaver rest

A dotted quaver usually pairs up with a semiquaver, since together they make up 1 crotchet beat:

dotted quaver
+
semiquaver

crotchet

The general effect of a passage like:

is of quavers with a "lilt."

Use the phrase **humpty dumpty** as a guide to this rhythm:

say: Hump-ty Dump-ty Hump-ty Dump-ty
        ▲   ▲   ▲   ▲
      stress   stress   stress   stress

These uneven types of rhythms are often called 'dotted rhythms'.

Look out for dotted rhythms in the next three pieces.

YELLOW SUBMARINE

Words & Music: John Lennon and Paul McCartney

SWING

20 Swing, a jazz style developed in the 1930's, is still popular today.

One of the main characteristics of swing is its use of lilting dotted rhythms. However, in Swing a phrase like:

say: hump-ty dump-ty
stress and hold back

would not be taken literally, but played in a more relaxed manner, like this:

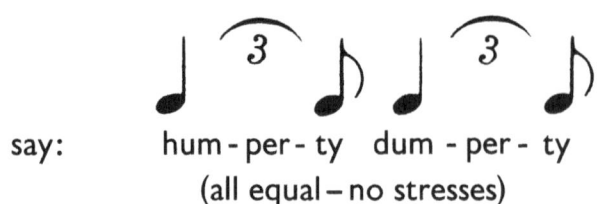

say: hum-per-ty dum-per-ty
(all equal – no stresses)

You will be playing these sorts of dotted rhythms in *Raindrops Keep Falling On My Head*, a modern tune written in the Swing idiom.

RAINDROPS KEEP FALLING ON MY HEAD
Words: Hal David. Music: Burt Bacharach

LAST WORD

So we come to the end of Book Three of *The Complete Piano Player*.

You are now familiar with the middle range of the piano, and Book Three has introduced you to some quite advanced timings and rhythm patterns.

In Book Four you will be:
- Learning more new notes
- Adding a little syncopation
- Playing in new keys
- Using the piano pedals
- Discovering new piano techniques

Till then your last song in this book is:

THE WONDER OF YOU
Words & Music: Baker Knight

© Copyright 1958 Duchess Music Corp., USA. MCA Music Ltd., for the world (exc. North, South and Central America, Japan, Australasia and the Philippines). All rights reserved. International copyright secured.